DUSTINA RESPECKI

LIVING IN FEAR AWAY FROM MY RAPIST

LIVING IN FEAR AWAY FROM MY RAPIST

DUSTINA RESPECKI

ISBN: 979-8-9880718-8-4

Printed in the United States of America

Published by

QUILL

info@thequippyquill.com
(302) 295-2278

CONTENTS

ACKNOWLEDGMENTS --------------------------------------- 1

Not the Same Person --------------------------------------29

Forever Changed ---30

All alone ---31

Not Yet ---32

ABOUT THE AUTHOR-------------------------------------35

ACKNOWLEDGMENTS

This story is based on a true story about friendship, leading to manipulation, to taking advantage of, to rape, and to putting the fear of everything in your heart and life.

Telling this story will hopefully help other women escape from their abusers.

When this kind of trauma is done to any one person, it becomes debilitating emotionally, mentally, spiritually, and physically. My advice is to go seek help.

My story starts way back in 1999. I live in Colorado Springs, Colorado, a city south of Denver, Colorado. It's a story about me being raped and being played dirty by someone I know.

It all started late that year. I was changing part-time jobs from the Village Inn to driving for Pizza Hut. I worked there two nights a week, sometimes three if they needed me to cover a shift or two. I really didn't mind if it was just once in a blue moon.

I started to get to know some of the people I worked with. There was Steve, Dustin, David, Russ, Amy, and Matthew, just to name a few who worked there.

So, after working there just a few weeks, sometime after I started, I think it was a Friday night because I closed the store that night.

Shortly after coming in to clock on for my shift, then came this guy, walked into the store through the employees' entrance. The sight of him pretty much punched me in the face, meaning he was pretty much a "Big Boy." There was not too much to say about him being there. I was pretty much shocked when I saw him.

After he clocked on for the night as well, he came up to me and asked if I was new at Pizza Hut. I said, "Well, yes. I started a few weeks ago. "Then I said, "I'm Dusty," but I never gave him my last name, but sooner than later, he found out (from what source, I don't know), which I thought was kind of creepy.

As the night went on, as we were in and out of the store, doing our job, I noticed him off and on staring at me as if he were caressing my body with his eyes.

I was trying so hard to not let him know I was noticing that he was staring at me as if he were interested in me and my body. Now I was really starting to wonder. I could not believe he was doing that. We just met. Then he would approach me at various times to just make small talk with him.

Some of the questions he was asking were a little personal to be asking someone. I was not thinking at that time but to answer. We just met, and I thought at that time some of them were too creepy to be asked in the first place, but I thought to myself it wouldn't hurt for him to ask, and I answered him back. So that is how we became friends and how all this nightmare got started.

Over the next few weeks, it about stayed constant with how he was doing things. You can tell he was getting obsessed over me, like an animal hunting in a way, from how he looked at me, to how he talked to me, to how his body language was when he was around me.

In the heat of the moment, it started confusing me. I was wondering why he was being that way and what was going through his mind. I probably will never know, but it really made me open my eyes some, but not enough, but I blew it off to a point.

But I was still trying to read into it. I felt as if I was putting too much energy into finding out what he intended to impose or throw my way. I didn't want him to know that I noticed that there might be something that was going on because I could not put my finger on it. So, I'd let him close one door, and I would wait for the other door to open. Just remember, I didn't know what he was planning, so I didn't say anything to him. Whenever it happened, it would come around, so I would step back and see what his crazy butt threw my way. I didn't let my wall go too high at that time because he would notice, but when I think about it now, I should have stacked it up higher.

During that time of my life, I was going through a separation from my ex-husband, Rod VDL. I would exit the marriage later with a divorce, so I was going through a lot of shit in my life and trying to make a life change for my daughter (Kirstin S.), and I did not know what was going to transpire.

I did not know what was going to start and take place with Mark S., which would be the beginning of a long road for me, not realize what would happen, but it would come to me as a complete shock to my life and for the rest of it.

It started out once a week when he would come up to me and ask me if he could ask me a question. I said sure, then he stood there a moment. Well, here it came out of his mouth, "Will you have sex with me?" I looked at him with a blank, shocked look, and I told him, "No, I'm not interested," and then he would walk away. He would ask me that at our place of employment, not realizing people were around. He did not care what they heard or thought, but of course, he didn't care about what I said to him. I knew he heard me, but he put it aside, not giving any care in the world because to him he was right.

He continued to ask me at work, then if I was working and he wasn't, he would take it upon himself to call the store and ask me, "Will you have sex with me?" I told him, "No, I'm not interested," then just like that, it happened so fast. It went up to two, three, four, or more times a week that he would ask.

He would not just ask me while we were on the clock or call me up while I was at work. He started calling me at home. I lived in an apartment at that time. I answered the phone. He asked me if I gave any thought of having sex with him. I told him no; I truly never gave him the thought that I wanted him.

While on the phone with him, I told him, "Mark, I don't know why you are finding it hard to understand. I don't want you. I did not give you the idea that I would have sex with you. "I told him, "I'm not interested." He really didn't want to hear me tell him that, then he said, "Please give it some thought."

Then that ended that conversation, and at that time, I hung up the phone.

Don't forget, it started out once a week to as much as four times a week after a while, and it didn't stop there. It would always be the same question, asking if I would have sex with him, asking me in every place you can ask someone, asking me that question in the parking lot at work. Then he showed up one night after closing the store. I was getting ready to leave. I was already pulled out of my parking place. He pulled up real fast with his dad being the one driving.

Then he asked, "Where are you going, Dusty?" I told him, "I'm going home."

Then of course he asked me the same damn thing. "Have you thought about it, having sex with me?"

I told him again, "No, I'm not interested. I got to get home." Then he pulled off something new. I ordered pizza from work to be delivered to my apartment. I got a knock at the door. Well, I knew that it should be the pizza that showed up.

When I opened the door, it came to me as a complete shock to see who was delivering the food. I looked at him and said, "Mark," then he gave me the total of my order, and I paid him and gave a tip as well. Then he made a remark and stated, "So this is where you live." In a sarcastic way, I paused and told him, "Yeah, and what about it?" He replied, "I always wanted to know where you lived." Then I replied, "Don't think about it."

Then here it came like clockwork. "Have you given it some thought of you and I having sex?"

I said for the hundredth time, "No, I'm not interested, so leave it alone."

He didn't look like he was really too happy with me after I said that, and then I got this look that just took the life right out of me. It was so horrifying to look at him, as if he were making a statement "How dare you tell me that?" And my feelings started raging out of control cause of the fear I felt out of it. To this day, I can't get over the look he gave. After that, it really surprised me in every way.

Then he was not just asking me while we were on the clock or out in the parking lot while waiting for me to come out so he could ask. He went as far as even calling my house phone to ask. Then I was thinking to myself, "Now he knows where I live."

I started to hide my car so he couldn't tell if I was home or not, and he still had a way of knowing that I was there. How he knew is beyond me. He started coming over to my house to ask me, and I kept on telling him, "No, I'm not interested," and he kept giving me that same evil look while I was closing the door.

As time went on, the fear I had was growing even more out of control to where I couldn't get the upper hand in taking back my feelings.

Now I had to keep my eyes open when I left the house to see where he was sitting, that is, if he was sitting somewhere nearby. I had thoughts of not knowing what was next in line for me.

The worry and the fear were consuming me now, not knowing what to do. He had my emotions riled up like a fish on a line. Mentally he was starting to wear me down with him continually asking me, the way he was doing it, and how often he was doing it.

He was getting very aggressive in the midst of it, showing he was going to win, showing he would take when you least expect it.

One day at dusk, I just got home, just walked in from being gone all day, not realizing to be on guard, hoping to have a quiet night without his bullshit.

No sooner than getting home, I spot his truck across the street, staring up at me. He was smoking a cigarette while looking at me out of the corner of his eyes, just piercing me with so much hate and despise.

You can tell he had been sitting there for some time, cause of the burned-out butts on the ground outside of his truck, just waiting and watching. Now I felt violated in the worst way. I was not even safe in my own home.

He kept asking me that dreadful question. "Have you thought about what we talked about, about us having sex?"

I looked at him. "Nope, don't really want to think about it. I'm not interested."

From the time this all started with him pushing me to the day he started to rape me had to be between eighteen to nineteen months.

The last time he asked me to have sex with him, we were at work, in front of everybody. They stopped and stared. Then once everybody went back to doing their thing, I looked at him and told him, "Let's get outside. I need to talk to you."

We went outside, to the back of the store. I asked him what his problem was. He told me, "All I want to do is have sex with you."

I told him, "Listen and listen very well. I'm only going to tell you this once. I'm getting tired of you asking me to have sex with you. No, I'm not interested. That means no, I don't want you. I'm done with telling you, and no, I'm not going to talk about it no more, and don't ever ask again."

Then he gave me that blank look he'd always given me.

Then days later, it would have been a Saturday, I had taken my daughter to a friend's house to sleep over, and then I headed home. I finally pulled into where I lived and parked my car, then I got out and was walking to the third floor of my apartment. I finally got to the front door and unlocked it. I entered the apartment, and then I closed the door and locked it. I went to place my stuff in my room. No more than five minutes had passed, and I got a knock at the door. Confused, I got to the door, then unlocked it to open it. I opened it enough to stick my head through, and I was shocked to see it was Mark S. at the door.

I asked, "What are you doing here? "Then he asked, "Can I come in?" Then I looked at him funny. I said no. I just walked in the door. and then he replied, "I know. I was sitting in the back parking lot behind the other building. I watched you leave with your daughter and saw you return." I stared at him in shock. I asked, "Are you stalking me?" "No, I'm not stalking you."

"It seems like it."

He told me, "Are you going to let me in?"

"No," I told him, "I have things to do." I started to close the door with him still outside.

Then he pushed the door open before I could get it closed all the way. I told him to leave, that I didn't want him at my apartment. He said, "No, I'm coming in." So, he walked right on in.

I said, "Leave, Mark, and do it now." He made it clear he was going nowhere, that he was there to get what he wanted. I still had the door open. He walked in and closed it, then he locked the door right behind him.

He looked at me with the dirtiest look. It really scared me really bad; that put the fear in me as well. I looked away and told him to go, and it started to get really bad.

He grabbed me by the arm and started to pull me into the bedroom. I pulled away and said no. He was not saying anything. He was giving me the look of evil, without putting his hands on me. I had my back toward my room. He started walking toward where I had no choice but to walk backward. I was trying to get away from him and to keep him from touching me. I tried to get around him, then he moved to the side I was trying to get through, and he started to push me with his huge body.

I started to cry, and I said no. He finally had me trapped in my room, and then he said, "I want to have sex with you. Do you realize how much I love you and want to be with you?"

I closed my eyes, shaking my head no. He started touching me. While he was doing that, I said, "No, no, you don't," while I was pushing him away.

I had tears rolling down my face, not knowing what I did to deserve this, wondering what to undress me. All I could do was try fighting him to keep my clothes on, then he grabbed hold of both of my hands with his right hand and pushed me against the wall to hold me still so he could pull my pants down,

He told me not to be loud to where people could hear, or something would happen to my daughter. I told him to keep her out of this.

"Just give me what I want and she will not get hurt."

Then when he had me pushed up against the wall, he moved in on me with my pants already down and off. He started to kiss my neck as I was crying, not just on the outside, but crying on the inside as well.

At this time, I was being broken spiritually, mentally, emotionally, and physically, stripped of being a woman, scared in and out. As he forced me to my bed, he still held my hands and arms so tightly together. He used his other hand and started from the top of me with my face, touching me to start getting his fill, then he went down to my neck, then he put his hand around my neck to keep me held down.

Then he went to kiss me. I was trying to turn my head so it couldn't happen, him laying his lips on mine.

What can you do when you're being raped? There is no way of getting up to run away when it's your house and bed he's doing that in. You lie there enduring the pain, the lashing.

Then he slid his free hand down to my breast, savagely scaring me and raping me, scratching and biting down to my navel. I squirmed, trying to get away. He held me even tighter to keep me from getting away.

Once he got to my female area, my body started to tremble with fear. I couldn't control myself. I couldn't stop. I told him to stop. He rubbed his fingers on my safe spot. I told him, "Please stop. Can't you hear me?" I tell him with words as I screamed on the inside as he continued. I was spinning in circles. I was out of control.

As I was lying there, I felt so nasty and gross, looking at him so disgustingly. I looked at him with fear and pain, and then the worst of this night was just getting started. He slid himself into my off-limits temple. He started to do it. Yes, I felt him thrusting himself inside of me. It started out slow to make sure he was fully there, then he went out of control. The thrusting was so hard. Oh god, it felt like I was being demolished and torn to pieces, and then I was trembling down, trembling like bad memories down a mountainside.

I was so terrified I wanted to scream. I wanted to die, the dirtiness I felt from him lashing my insides.

When he was lashing my insides, I was losing my mind. These feelings were like a bad nightmare that had been going on for days but was only a mere few hours. I whispered to him to please stop, please go.

After he destroyed me, I lay there curled up on my bed, hoping my world would stop spinning. As he got dressed, he told me, "That was great. It makes me want you even more. Was it good for you as it was for me?" I never answered.

After he left, I jumped into the shower to wash off. Maybe I should have not done that, but I felt nasty and violated. He destroyed my insides and outside. Once I had my shower done, I had to leave the apartment to get away. Was I scared to leave my home after that? Yes. I looked out all my windows to see where he was. I couldn't see him. I even looked down the halls of my apartment. They were outdoor halls. I walked down to the end of the hallway to see if he was parked out back. He was nowhere around, so I ran to my car to get in and get out of there. I was afraid he would come back.

At this time, I had jumped in my car so I could get out of there for a while. I was driving down the street, not really going to any place special, but to drive to clear my mind and soak in what had just happened.

I thought to myself, "How am I going to work with him and deal with what just happened? I can't quit. I need my job. I have no choice but to live with it."

The next time I went to work, I hoped to be able to take being around him.

When it came to work, it was hard to be around him. I made sure I was around other people at work so I would not feel so awkward. He would give me the look of evil, the look of hate I called it. He did it so he could keep me down in every which spiritually broken, mentally battered, and afraid to look at him. He had me trapped between hell and reality. When he had the chance to see me alone, he would say things that crossed me as being mean things to say to me or anyone.

You never knew when he would come over to rape me some more. It was spontaneous usually; it happened when my daughter was not around. He knew when she was gone because he was watching. He was stalking me. I never knew when or where he could be sitting.

But for sure, he knew when I came home and left. When he was watching, regardless if I saw him or not, I felt violated. How can I live my life happily when I'm in constant fear? Remember, ever since he raped me, the first time, he said he would show up spontaneously. It happened about every six to eight weeks, and every time he raped me, it felt even worse and more vulgar.

My mind was spinning out of control more and more each day. I had to find some way to get him to stop. Every time he started to touch, or kiss, I said no, then he got more aggressive, more powerful, more controlling.

All the mental, physical, emotional, and spiritual abuse that had been done, it was going on too long, too many years it felt like an eternity, but to sum it up, it only lasted over two years since the first attack of rape, starting in April of 2001 to April of 2003.

In May of 2003, I met Dave, who now is my husband today in 2016. I met him on May 12, 2003, but the abuse I endured with Mark S. will not end here.

Dave and I clicked real fast and started mating. He would come out every weekend from Flagler, Colorado. He would be here from Friday night till

Sunday night, then he would go back home because he would have to return back to work.

One weekend in June of 2003, mid to late morning, we were leaving out the door from my apartment to go spend the day outdoors. My apartment door was tucked away at the end of the outside hall near the street, and then we all walked down the hall to turn down the other hall to make our way toward the stairs. We all were looking straight ahead. I said out loud, "I'll be damned." It was Mark S.

I turned to Dave, and he said, "What is wrong? Do you know him?" I stated, "Yes," and then I said, "Please take the kids downstairs to the car and I will be with you. If I'm not down there in five to six minutes, call the police and only you come up and get me."

"OK, don't take too long."

Mark S. and I waited till they got in the car, and Mark S. said, "Who is he?"

I told him, "He is my boyfriend and we're talking about moving in together as soon as possible."

Then he just went to be very quiet, then he looked as if the life ran out of him, from shock to look at me as if he was going to grab me by the neck and choke the very life out of me. Then all of a sudden, he said in a hurtful way, "How can you do this to me?"

I looked at him in a way like, "What do you mean how can I do this to you?"

Then he went.

"Excuse me," I told him, "You act like we're dating, like I'm all yours, that nobody else can have me to claim for their own."

Then he started reacting very aggressively toward me, then he made the remark and made the mistake stating, "You are mine."

I looked at him with a face of disgust and then said, "I'm done with this. I can't take this anymore. I'm done, Mark." I started to go around him to walk toward the stairs, and then he put himself in front of me so I wouldn't go anywhere, like every time before when he raped me. He started to push me backward toward my apartment and said, "You are mine, not his. I'm going to take you back into your apartment and make love to you."

I stopped him and looked at him with a mean face and said, "Mark, you call it what you want you call that lovemaking or any kind of feeling of love. I told Dave if I'm not downstairs in the car in five to six minutes to call the police and to come and get me."

Then he stepped aside, then I started to walk away, then he made a remark by saying, "So Dave is his name."

I turned around and looked at him. He looked at me, waiting for an answer. He was crying. I didn't say anything to him, so I just proceeded to walk down the stairs.

I finally reached the car and got in. While we were leaving, Dave asked, "What did he want?"

I said to Dave, "Don't worry about it. I don't want to say it in front of the kids. What he wants he really needs to understand. I can't give him it anymore. I've been telling him for many years to leave it alone."

In July of 2003, I moved out of my apartment. We temporarily moved into a house till we closed on our house. At this time, I was transferring my house phone to the new house while we were finalizing the paperwork, so there was no way for Mark S. to get in touch with me other than at work until I moved into my house. Then all of a sudden, out of the blue, I was getting calls from Mark. I could not believe that he was doing the calling thing again, but even then, he was being somewhat quiet with me.

When he would talk to me over the phone, he would try to make me feel guilty. "I can't believe you're doing this. "I just rolled my eyes, but if we were on the phone, I would hang up on him, but of course, he gave me that look that he always gave me, that he controlled me when he was in front of me. He was not quite getting it. I didn't understand why he still thought he had control over me.

You got to remember, during the time between April 2003 to August 2009, there was no physical rape, just the mental, emotional, and spiritual rape going on, but he was keeping me abused in these ways.

So, knowing at that time, there was still the fear of it all, plus him possibly doing the sexual abuse again.

Then around the middle to late September of 2003, I left Pizza Hut for good to go work for McDonald's. At this time, Mark S. and I were only on speaking terms. Why he wouldn't stop calling me, I didn't know. If I hung up, he called back. I was not going to change my number just because of him. From September 2003 till the end of the year, we did talk some.

I was kind of relieved to not hear from him all the time. Usually, he was keeping a tight squeeze on me. I really needed to work on myself but was having a terrible time doing just that, because of him continuing the calls. My mind is wandering back, to what he was doing to me. I try to make sense of it, but who knows if I ever will.

Let's jump to February 2004. I haven't heard from Mark, which was good. No, I was not wanting him to call. What I'm saying is, he was very controlling. This is the month Dave asked me to marry him. Then a month later, I ended up pregnant. Within a few months, after I found out I was pregnant, we got married.

Sometime in July of 2004, I got a call from Mark S. I was shocked to hear from him; it had been months. I asked him what he needed. He said, "Is there a problem with me calling a friend?"

I said, "No."

Then he asked how I had been. "Everything has been good." He asked if I was still with Dave. "Well, of course. Why do you ask?" "Because I miss you." me.

I said, "Mark, we are not going to start down this road of manipulating" He went, "I'm not."

I told him we got married this past June. "And why do you really need to know?"

"Just asking."

I guess he was feeding into my answer because he was really wanting to know more about my last fifteen months with Dave because he never asked me a whole lot about it.

I was as confused as any person would be. He had gone silent while on the phone with me. I said, "Are you there?"

"Yes," then he told me he had to go. I said, "OK, bye."

Sometime the next month, I got a call on my cell phone midmorning. I said, "Hello."

He went, "Hey."

I told him, "What do you need?" He wanted me to come over. I told him, "I don't know. I really feel funny about doing that," but really, I still had a lot of fear inside me. I stepped back to give some light on the fact that he had raped me. It just seemed like I couldn't get loose and run away. He begged and begged me to come over to see him and visit. I was five months pregnant at that time. I got to the point I got sick of hearing him ask, so I went over to see him, knowing it was not a good idea to do so, but he would not leave it alone.

I went to see him. I asked, "So what do you want to visit about or talk about?"

Then he came right out and said, "Can we go upstairs so we can be together sexually?"

I looked at him and said, "Is that the reason you wanted me over here? To ask me to be with you sexually?"

He went, "Yes. If I had told you over the phone, you would not have come over, plus I wanted to see you."

I said, "You know I'm married and I'm pregnant." He said, "It does not stop me from wanting you."

"You know how long it's been since I have had sex," I said. "I really don't care how long it's been."

"It's about time for me to go."

He went, "Can I see your butt? Can you pull down your pants for me?" I said no. I picked up my stuff and walked out the door. I couldn't believe he called me over for this. Since me being at his house and leaving his house, we probably talked to each other every three to four weeks, just so he could keep his manipulation and control on me, and he would ask me lots of questions so he could use them against me, at that time not knowing he was doing the manipulation. I was not picking up on it that well. At the time, it felt like being in a trance when you are under the control of someone that is so good at manipulating, not just you, but everybody around him. I'm no doctor, but he showed signs of some kind of mental problems, not just on me, but also on other women and men. He showed no remorse. He would lie and be two-faced at the same time. He was doing all this for his own benefit. Like I said, I felt like I was in a trance. It was like being drugged. I could not escape from all of his controlling ways over me. I did not know right from wrong but felt something was out of place. I could not put a finger on it.

All through 2005, he and I were just talking on the phone. I didn't go to his house that year because of what happened before, and to think about it, even over the next three years and nine months, I hadn't visited his house.

Then from 2005 to August 2009, I passed him on the streets. Back in time, in June of 2006, to be exact, we ran into each other in the K-Mart parking lot. We sat there for about an hour or so, talking, plus he was slipping in a question here and there during the conversation. He was asking questions about my husband, step kids, and what side of town I lived on.

Close to the end of our conversation, he started playing his games, and some of them were without making it look like he was trying to throw me off to keep me in the conversation to keep it going.

He said, "How can you leave me like that?" All I did was look down and shake my head, thinking to myself, I should have seen it coming.

He said, "You hurt me really bad, and I'm still hurting from it, plus I hate your husband for taking you from me. "I looked at him with a face of disgust, and then he went, "What, does a man have rights to his feelings?" I told him, "Yes, but keep me out of it," then I heard those crazy words I didn't want to hear come out of his mouth. "I'm in love with you. I want you back."

I looked at him and told him, "I'm sorry you feel that way, but you can't be serious about loving me. "Then he gave me a look, the look of I should be afraid, and told me not to tell him how he should feel for me. Then I told him, "I have to go. I have things to do."

Between that encounter and July 3, 2008, he and I went to talking on the phone a couple of times a month. We also passed each other on the streets from time to time. The phone conversations at this point in time had more discussions of him wanting me back and what he wanted to do to me. I told him to change the subject cause I was not interested in doing anything of the sort, and if he did not change the subject, I was going to have to get off the phone with him because it made me feel uncomfortable, so he kept going on about what I told him not to talk about. So, I told him I got to go, I needed to get off the phone. This is that part where he heard me but did not care to stop. Every time after that, he kept it up and told me not to hang up, and then he started to threaten me a little. It was at this point in time when I thought he would have changed. Then on July 4, 2008, he called me up and asked if I could come up to see him at his job site up Dublin and Powers.

I asked him why because I hadn't seen him in a while, then I told him, "Understand one thing. Don't do anything stupid or say anything stupid, 'cause I will have my son with me."

He said, "OK," so I went over to see him. I really didn't know what was going on in my mind to do this crazy stuff. When I got there, I stayed outside of his truck. He had got out and walked to the back of the truck to where I was standing. We started to talk, and then he came up beside me, right beside me. Then he grabbed my butt and whispered in my ear, "I want you bad. When can we be together again?"

At that moment, I looked at him and said, "I don't want to be with you like that. "Then he just started acting crazy. I could not believe how he was acting. I said, "I told you not to act this way."

Then he said, "Be what way?"

I shook my head and said, "You got to be kidding me. I told you not to start or I was not going to come. "Then I left because I was going to meet up with my husband. He drove a truck, so he was coming home for a day.

From this day in July of 2008 till June 2009, it went back to just talking like it had been done in the past. I was full of nothing but fear of what he could be stewing up to do to me.

Because it was just too confusing to me why he didn't get the clue that I didn't want him, but it just seemed to go through one ear and out the other. He knew what I was saying but really didn't care what I got to say about him, leaving me alone on wanting to be with me sexually. Sometime before the summer of 2009, it was sometime that spring, I told Dave, my husband, I would like to drive for the local cab company to make some extra money.

So, we started getting our stuff together to start doing that while he was still driving a semi. June came around. I think it was around the ninth of June of 2009. We took the class and went out driving with another driver for training.

Dave took his semi back up to Wyoming to give them a week's notice. That following Friday, we were out driving. I started doing the night shift, so I could spend my first night doing the bar rush. After the bar rush, I decided to book in to take one last run, so I received a run somewhere downtown off some street just south of Platte Avenue.

I picked up a woman from her house and asked where she was wanting me to take her. She said she was calling to find out. I turned around to head back to Platte Avenue because I was just south of it.

While I was doing that, she was calling the person that she was going to see.

When she had the person on the phone, you could tell she was talking to a man by the way they were talking. By what she was saying, you could tell what he was saying to her; it sounded all too familiar.

I was starting to have some really bad anxiety starting to surface because I was already wondering whom she was talking to. It was already going through my head. Then she asked me, "Do you know where the Wendy's is on Powers and Palmer Park Boulevard?" I said yes, and then she gave me more info about whom she was going to see. Then she said, "You know that street to the left past that Wendy's, there are some warehouses there." I said yes, and then she said, "That is where we are going. "Then they hung up with each other.

Within a minute or two, I was getting a call from Mark S. I was shocked that he would be calling me while I was at work. I was getting the feeling she was talking to him. I answered the phone and said, "Hello. "Then he went, "It's me."

I said, "OK, what do you want?"

Then he went, "The woman you have in your car is coming to see me. Do you understand where I'm at?"

"Yeah."

"When I see you, I will flash my lights."

I said, "OK," and then I hung up with Mark and started to talk to the passenger. Her name was Lisa. I said, "I didn't know you knew Mark S." She said, "I met him about a year ago."

I told her that was interesting, then I told her, "Just be careful with him. I would keep an open eye on him.

She chuckled and said, "I will."

Around 3:00 a.m. that morning, I finally got her to where Mark S. was located. She got out of the cab and got up into his truck, then he got out of the truck and walked up to me to pay for the cab ride. I said, "Mark S., shame on you."

He went, "Well, you won't give me what I want out of you." I asked, "And what do you mean by that?"

"I want you back sexually. I want to be inside you, loving you only. You're mine. Do you think I want to go as low as being with her? The only reason I'm fucking her is she owes me a lot of money, and this is how she is paying me back."

I said, "Mark, you disappoint me. Whatever floats your boat, Mark." When he saw that I was driving a cab, he really started keeping in touch with me from June 2009 to August 2009. It was weekly that he was calling me, wanting me around more and more. I was really starting to worry about him and what he might do, with the way he was acting toward me.

Then in August 2009, it went full-blown. It went daily. I was starting to get really worried, more traumatized, and more withdrawn, and then he went to being demanding and wanting to see me on a daily basis. If I never showed, he called, blowing up my phone to make sure I was coming. If I didn't answer, he would get some balls to call dispatch to locate my car. I could not believe it. When I found out that he was acting like my husband to get the info, I would call him up and tell him to stop calling the office to locate my cab.

He asked, "Why are you not over in this area of town?"

I told him, "Do you hear me? Stop calling them to see where I am." He said, "Then start answering your phone and I won't call anymore." So, in order to get him to stop, I had no choice but to do as he told me. He worked as a security guard at night, 7:00 p.m. to 6:00 a.m., Wednesday to Sunday for about nine months. He was guarding some of the motor city lots.

Every night he worked; he expected me to be there after I was done with working the cab because he wanted to count how much I made. Saturdays were different. I started out a lot earlier. He also worked at Pizza Hut once he was done driving. I had to go with him to this gas station to hang out for a while.

After he demanded me to stop by both jobs and all, he had a new game plan on how he was going to manipulate me. It was worse than before. Remember September of 2003 to August of 2009, when we were just talking on the phone plus the few times we saw each other and talked, those questions he asked about my husband and stepkids. At this time, this is where he put all that into play, to get me to have sex with him, for him to get what he wanted to rape me again. The words, the threats were even worse. They were really starting to really scare me, lashing at me and ripping me apart. The wounds were open; the wounds were deep.

So of course, there were also the using and the downright awful threats. This is what's going to happen. One Friday night, at the beginning when he was wanting me, after I was done with work, I was scared of course, drained, and tired. I went from my cab to his car. We drove around Motor City, then we went to this spot of the property called the Overflow. That is where they kept extra cars. Up in the Overflow, it was very dark, maybe one light up there.

Then we parked, then he shut the lights off so no one could find out where we were sitting (I wish someone would have). This is where the sexual abuse started, shortly after he wanted me up there with him at his job.

I would be sitting in the passenger seat in the front seat of his work car. He would touch my leg near the knee. I would tell him to stop and push his hand away, and then he looked at me with such hate, and every time, it would scare me so badly. I didn't know why it did, then he started doing it again. He would work his hand up my left thigh on the inside. I said, "Mark, stop." He kept on doing it. He finally reached my private spot, my secret area. My eyes started to tear up.

I told him, "No, I'm not here for that." He heard but didn't care to stop doing what he was doing. You could tell by the look he gave me; he proceeded to touch me. He told me to not think about running, and that he would do something to my husband or to one of my step kids.

It had gotten to be a ritual with him touching me, him putting his hands on my secret place, me squirming out of hate for what he was doing, asking me for money left and right. The touching turned into violating me by forcing himself on me. Sometimes he would rape me in a hidden place outside somewhere. Who knows who could have been watching, or the buildings' cameras could have been seeing us. There were several times. He would tell me to come over to his house, and if I refused, he would start to threaten me. To keep things from getting out of hand, I did as he wanted, knowing I didn't want anything to do with what he was doing to me.

When he would rape me, he would pull my hair, slap me, stick his fist up inside of me, then he would violate me by putting himself up inside my rectum. When he did that, it felt so bad, like I was being ripped apart, more like shredding me apart. I was screaming so hard within me because the people next door would hear me if I were to scream out loud.

In June of 2010, he was demanding me to move into this apartment that he and I got. He wanted me to go as far as filing for divorce and wanted me to change my last name to his.

During this time, he wanted me to take my husband's rights away from him so I could give him the rights to my son Joe. I told him, "I can't do that. I have to show proof that he is an unfit parent, and there is no way I can prove it."

This is one way he was controlling me. The threats had been getting worse and worse. There were times he would bring up that he could get rid of my stepkids and my husband. I said, "Why would you do that? I don't want anyone killed."

"Cause I don't like any one of them, and Dave stole you from me." Then he said, "I have a friend here that has family that can come and help. All they have to do is drive up here from the south and help me get rid of them. All I have to do is pay these people to come up here and beat the shit out of them and put bags over their heads and take them down to Louisiana state and feed them to the crocs."

I told him he needed to stop. "I don't want to hear it. I don't want nobody dead at all." But he kept bringing it up from time to time, not leaving it alone. Then he had his friend tell me over the phone numerous times when I was around Mark; his friend told me that Mark had talked to him about doing away with my two younger stepkids and my husband, plus he also talked about it in front of me as well, and he was very serious about getting the job done when needed.

I just could not believe what I was hearing coming out of Mark's and his friend's mouths, and that they were planning all this stuff to do with three people's lives. I asked his friend what they were going to plan so I could get the two stories straight and see if they were saying the same thing. I was just shocked over all this shit. Still, I told those two idiots they were crazy, damn crazy.

I went back to my car, and I got into it and I left. Mark called and asked me, "Why did you leave? Where did you go?"

"I told you I don't want you talking about that stuff of killing people. I don't want to hear you talking about that stuff about you hurting anybody. Don't get me involved with any of that."

There was a time in the late summer of 2010. He wanted to open his own security company and wanted me to help him with running it. I told him, "OK, let's plan it." He told me to make a plan to get a gun bought. During this time, I put a 9 mm gun on layaway. By the beginning of December of 2010, I had got the gun off layaway. I had kept the gun at my house for a few days. I really didn't feel right about keeping the gun at my house.

Mark said, "You can store it at my house." So, I took it over to his house a day or two later. We put the gun in his garage. We put it in this empty box that was out there, and then after that, I had to leave. During this time, he had gotten even worse at manipulating me because he had my gun. The raping was even nastier as time went on. I was getting even more withdrawn from myself. I was getting more depressed, not having any way to stop it.

Around April of 2011, I was telling my babysitter Tammy about how I allowed Mark to hold on to my gun. Tammy knew who Mark was. She made a statement to me by saying, "What the hell is your problem? Why did you let him hold on to your gun?"

I told her, "I was not thinking. I guess I thought it was right at the time, that he would hold on to it for me."

So, she was discussing with me a plot on how we could get my gun back from Mark S. I told her I was planning on just walking out of his life and getting away because I was fed up with his shit and the games he was playing. Then she said, "You better do more than that."

Around the beginning of June 2011, I started to confront him while I was at his job site by saying, "Hey, Mark, I need my gun back." I was asking him every so often for my gun. He would say to me with such a look "Why are you asking?" by saying, "Why?"

"Because I need it."

He would answer, "No, your younger stepson will get to it and kill you with it, or you will shoot yourself with it."

I said to him, "My stepson moved out, and no, I won't do myself in. Where do you get this crazy shit in your head in the first place?" Then weeks later, I asked for my gun again. He kept giving me the same line again. "No, you're not going to get it back 'cause your stepson will get a hold of it and kill you, or you will kill yourself with it."

I had been asking for the gun back for a year now. I was talking with my babysitter Tammy about what Mark was saying. She said, "I'm telling you, Dusty, you have to get the sheriff's department involved to save yourself some heartache, and also getting yourself in trouble." I told her, "I'm trying, but I'm scared of what he might do." She went, "I'm just trying to save your butt."

I said, "I know, I will get it done."

In March of 2012, apparently, I said something wrong in his eyes. In my eyes I said nothing wrong. I told him what I felt. For three days he did not say anything to me at all. I texted him and asked if he was mad at me. I knew he really was. He still didn't answer me. Just to get him to say something, I told him I was not going to go to my doctor's appointment in April up in Denver. Then he said something by text. He told me, "If you ever talk to me like that again, you will pay for it." Then he replied and said, "You can make up for it. "I said, "How?" "You can meet me at my job site and find out. "I asked, "What are you asking of me to do?"

He said, "I'm still thinking about what your punishment is."

I knew he had it all thought out already and was playing his mind games with me.

When it finally became dark outside, I headed over there to see him. He always wanted me to wait till it got dark outside so the cameras on the building could not see me. When I arrived, he was standing behind the car, leaning up against it. I got out of my car and walked up to where he was. He was smoking a cigarette, and he was giving me that cross-eyed look he always gave me when he was disgusted with something I did or said.

Then he said "Come closer" 'cause I was standing out of arm's length. Out of fear of what he might do to me if I didn't, I went closer to him like he wanted me to, and then he grabbed me and pushed me up against the car to where I was facing it. I tried turning around to look at him, to ask him why he was doing this. He kept me pinned there while he was pulling my pants down. I was trying to bend down to grab my pants. He wouldn't let me, then he grabbed my waist and pulled me toward him. I was saying, "Will you stop?" He said no. He got to that point where he entered me. I was trying to push him away so I could get my pants pulled up and get the hell out of there. I sure did not like what was going on at that point, then he went, "Let those pants go. You're not going anywhere." He put his foot on my pants so I could not reach them, and he entered me again and started thrusting in me fast and hard.

I told him, "No, this is wrong." He kept going. After ten minutes, he released himself inside of me. Then at that time, I pulled my pants up walked away, and left. He yelled, "Where are you going?" I didn't say anything to him, and I got in my car and drove off. I left there just in so much shock and was thinking to myself that this was my punishment for this and was thinking, "If this is what it is going to turn into for everything I do wrong, then I'm in trouble."

This stuff with the gun kept going on till June of 2012, with me trying to get my gun back. Then Tammy told me on a Thursday in June of 2012, "Why don't you tell him I bought the gun and that I gave you $600 for it and that you used it to pay some bills, that I need to get the gun by Sunday because I needed it to give it to my grandson because they were leaving to go out of state."

So that night, I went to his job site and said, "Mark, I need my gun." He said, "Why?"

I said, "You remember my babysitter Tammy?"

He said yes. I then told him that she paid me $600 for it and I needed to give it to her by Sunday. "She is giving it to her grandkids as a gift, 'cause they are going to be leaving the state in the next few weeks." He said, "OK, I'll get it for you."

Sunday came around. I had this gut feeling when I was driving over there that he did not have it. I got there to where he worked. I said, "Hey, do you have the gun? "Then he told me it was in his garage, that he was still looking for it. I started to think he really didn't look for it, then this was the time he started to act really funny and really shady. So, I looked at him and said, "Mark, we put it in a box inside your garage."

He said, "I know. It's a matter of what box it is in."

Then I said, "You better not have done nothing with my gun, Mark, or I'm going to be so mad."

He just looked at me like "Whatever." And how he looked at me, it took me down so bad I was like a little puppy with my tail between my legs.

I told him, "I'll be back. I'm going to text Tammy to see what she thinks."

Then he went, "Why would you do that?"

"Well, she needs to know you didn't find it. "I texted her and told her what was being said and transpiring on my end. She said, "Dusty, you better get the police involved. Something smells rotten." But then she told me, "Tell him I'll give him till Thursday to get you the gun to give to me."

So, I walked back to where Mark was and said, "She will give you till Thursday to give me the gun, so I can give it to her."

He said, "OK. I'll get it found and give it to you then."

When Thursday came around, I went to Mark's job site and said, "So where is my gun? "Then the stupid ass had the damn nerve to tell me that there was a possibility that he could've thrown the gun away. I looked at him so funny and was dumbfounded, then I turned around and looked away, then I turned back to look at him and said, "How in the hell can you throw my gun away? Are you crazy?"

Then he looked at me cross-eyed like he always had done. I told him, "I have to go and think about this. "Then he started acting really funny. He said, "What is there to think about?"

I told him, "You just told me you threw my gun away. How do you want me to act? It seems kind of funny to throw something like that away."

So, I walked away to my car to get in and drive away to go home. I was so upset I could not sleep that night. He texted me and said, "I don't understand why you left. "I could not believe what he just said. I said, "Mark, you just told me you threw my gun away. I really don't want to talk right now because you acting really stupid right now."

Then sometime that weekend after that, I found out that he threw it away. I had talked to Tammy about it. She looked at me with a disgusted look and said, "What did I tell you to do?" I told her that I would do as she had asked me to do-to call the cops.

She went, "You really need to listen and do as I say. I know you really don't want to get him into trouble. I know you are afraid of him, but I don't want you in trouble. If someone gets their hands on that gun and does something stupid with it, you will be the one in trouble with the crime." So, I really thought it through. It was on Father's Day in 2012. I called the El Paso County Sheriff's Office and told them I needed a deputy to come out so I could talk to him about my gun. One showed up, and I told him the story about my gun. After talking with him, he went out to his car and called Mark S. He came back into the house moments later. He said, "I just got off the phone with Mr. Mark S. He gave me the same story you gave me. Here is my card with the case number on it. He said the gun is in his garage. Give him some time to find it. If he does not produce it, then call me back up and I will take care of it for you."

Later that night, he texted me and said, "Why did you call the cops on me?"

"Mark, I told you I would call them if you didn't give me the gun back. I'm serious about this. I'm really wanting my gun back. "Then he told me, "It's in my garage."

I was like, "Why did you tell me it's your garage then you tell me you threw it away, now it's back in your garage?"

Between June 17, 2012, and August 19, 2012, I was really getting on him to get me my gun, and then he went, "I'm still looking for it."

I told Mark, "You haven't started to even look for the gun. You're sitting on your couch doing nothing but watching TV."

So August 19, 2012, I had enough and called the cop back and gave him the case number, and he looked it up. He said, "I remember this call." I told him, "He never looked for the gun. All he is doing is giving me the runaround, so can you do a pawnshop check for me?"

He says he would do so. He said he would call me back when he found out anything about what was going on with it. I said, "OK, have a nice day."

On August 26, 2012, the cop called me back and told me, "I can't believe he lied to me. He pawned it in May of 2011, and the gun was sold in July of 2011."

I said to the cop, "I told you when you were here at my house in June that he is a liar."

Then the cop told me, "Don't act no different around him. Don't see him less, 'cause I'm going to work on getting a warrant for his arrest. Why I'm telling you not to act different or see him any less, he will pick up on it."

So that night, I went to his job site. He went, "What's up?" I told him, "Not too much. Same thing, different day."

He went, "So what are you doing standing on the passenger side of the car and not standing on my side of the car?"

I said, "Because I want to. "Then he started to act funny, real funny. Then I said, "Mark, what's wrong? What's on your mind?" He was giving me that same damn evil eye like I was up to something.

Then he said, "I'm feeling something is going on."

Then I told him, "By all means, what are you talking about? I'm very confused."

He gave me an attitude. "Come on, Dusty, you must know something."

I looked at him with a straight face. "About what?"

"For some reason, you're on that side of the car. You don't tell me you love me anymore, and you're not talking about your gun anymore." I told him, "Well, I told you I want to be on this side of the car. Two, do I have to tell you every time I see you that I love you?" He really started getting mad. "And three, I really don't want to talk about the gun. I'm getting that taken care of."

Then he went, "What do you mean by that?"

Then I told him, "Just what I told you. I'm taking care of it. Don't worry about it, just change the story please."

Then it came to that time when the cop called him-the date was September 20, 2012, and told him there was a warrant for his arrest, that he had till September 30, 2012, to turn himself in, or they would come to his house to arrest him. Then later that day, he contacted one of our friends that we shared by text message. It was the same day he was told to turn himself in within ten days. The day was September 20, 2012. He told Jason about what had happened, and then Jason asked Mark, "Does this have anything to do with Dusty's gun, Mark?"

Mark said, "Yes."

Jason said to him, "Mark, you did her wrong, and you know that." Mark never replied on that part of doing me wrong, knowing that Jason just got telling him he did me wrong. He really didn't want to hear that. Then he went straight for the kill. Mark asked Jason to help him get out of trouble. Jason said, "Man, I can't help you. I put my hands down to you. Did you not hear me? You did her wrong, and I don't want to be involved in helping you, even in helping you wrong her even more."

That same day after Mark asked Jason for help, Jason sent me a text that Mark sent him. I was just dumbfounded by what Mark was saying to Jason and why he was trying to get out of trouble by using other people to help him, but of course, that was part of his problem.

Mark was busy that whole day. Later that night, Mark texted me and asked me why I called the police on him. I said, "Mark, you got to be kidding me. You pawned my gun. What did you want me to do? Not turn you in? What you did was wrong in all ways." Then he told me that he thought I would understand why he pawned it, that I should have not turned him in, that it was my fault that he was in trouble. I told him, "I can't believe what I'm hearing. "I asked him, "Are you saying it's OK to pawn my stuff for money to benefit yourself?"

Mark stated, "You ruined my life."

I told him, "No, you did only you, and you will pay for what you did. "Then he said, "Don't ever call me again."

I should be the one saying that to him.

Then at this time, I was just waiting for word on his arrest or seeing if he turned himself in. The call came in the evening of September 30, 2012, that he didn't turn himself in, and that they were going out the next day to arrest him in the wee hours of the morning.

I got a call the next morning at 8:00 a.m. to be told they made an arrest. I was so happy and jumping for joy. Then he was let out on bond on October 1, 2012. They were trying to figure out if they should have a jury trial or a plea deal. He took the plea. The plea was that they would drop the theft charges, but he had to take a theft class. But he was charged with a felony for lying to a pawnbroker, plus two years' probation, and he had to pay me restitution of about $650. This all was made law on December 4, 2012.

During the next few months, I received three checks with different amounts but adding up to $650. I was just happy to get it.

Since I hadn't talked to or seen him, I knew it seemed weird to say this, but when you're being abused in so many ways mentally, emotionally, and physically bring you spiritually down. You know it's wrong on all parts of what they're doing to you, but it seems like you can't live without them.

Between September 2012 to July 2013, I was having a very hard time emotionally keeping myself together, so I called Tessa to seek some help for the raging emotions I was having. So late July of 2013, I started going to Tessa to talk to a counselor. During this time, I had called the sheriff's office to turn Mark S. in for the rape. Before, I was afraid to do it cause of the fear I had within me because of him putting it there from all the abuse he was doing to me.

I started going on Tuesdays to see someone for counseling, so when I started to deal with the sheriff's office, I had to be called in to be questioned about everything that took place. I guess it took about an hour or so for all the questioning.

Then after about eighteen months had gone by, I started seeing Mark S. everywhere I went, I was just done in for. I started feeling like he was following me, then there were times he would stare at me with a pissed-off look as if he was going to attack me if he could. Then when we would pass, he would try hiding his face as if he were the victim. I just shook my head in disappointment.

Now getting back to what I was talking about to the sheriff's office. He had Mark S. in to talk to him and ask him some questions about what was going on. Prior to having him in, the detective told me that Mark S. would do one of those numbers that I said. He said that in situations like this, they all do when they're being put on the spot on a rape complaint. Then he said, "Don't get upset about it." I told him I wouldn't.

The detective had him in interrogation for well over two hours. The detective called me up the same day to tell me what was said and asked of Mark. Some of the questions the detective asked Mark S. were, "How many times did you conduct sexual activities with the victim?" He stated thirty times. "How far apart was each time?" He couldn't remember that, plus I told the detective when I first started to talk to him that I was seeing a counselor as well, and he asked for her number. Sometime in the next few days, he called her to ask questions. This took place before he talked to Mark S.

Yes, I'm going to bounce back and forth a little. Shortly before the calls to the police about him raping me and before he had gotten in trouble for the gun, he would text me. One day he texted what he was going to do to me sexually. He had explained it in so much detail that it would scare me. I stopped texting him for the rest of the night. Then hours later, I was getting some more texts from Mark. I was wondering why he was texting me. I really did not want to talk 'cause of what he was saying. I opened up the text to read it. It stated, "Who is this?" It seemed kind of funny why Mark would be texting me that. I said, "Don't play with me you know who this is."

"This is not the person you were talking to earlier."

I said, "Don't play games with me. "Then I found out I was talking to Mark's wife.

She went, "You know he's married."

I said, "Yes, I know, and I'm married as well. I'm only Mark's friend." Then she started, "Why is there sexual stuff being said in your guy's text for?"

Then I told her, "If you noticed, the things that are being said sexually are coming from him. Don't put me as saying them. Yes, they are addressed to me. I never said anything sexually back to him, so you need to rip him. I don't want him in that way. He's not my type." The conversation ended there.

Back to the investigation on Mark raping me. The detective was talking to him and done contacting me. He wrote his report up to give to the DA's office. About a week later, he called me to tell me he submitted the report to the DA's office, then he told me if I didn't hear from them in a week, to call him up and he would get on them.

A week passed. I called the detective and left a message on his answering machine.

About three or four days later, I received a letter in the mail stating that they believed that he had done the act that I turned him in for, that I needed some more stuff on him, for what he did, for a jury. So, once I could get something together, then they would be more than happy to prosecute him.

I never had a rape kit done. I was too scared of what he was capable of doing to me from hurting me, to hurting my family. Who knows? He could not be trusted, so I gave it up, hoping that karma would come around soon enough.

So early 2014, I started seeing him around town even more (yes, I was running into him). At this time, I was starting to panic more and more. It had got to be really bad. It was happening on a daily basis that the anxiety was happening. It felt like I was dying emotionally and even in every other way. I was starting to go downhill real fast, then he spotted me, giving me the look, he always gave me, like he was going to do something, the look of wanting to kill me.

Like I said before, when I would pass him on my side of the car, he would cover his face so I wouldn't see him. I was starting to think, "What, are you scared of me? I'm just in a car." I did nothing to him like he thought I did. At the time, I just wanted to be friends. That was not good enough for him. After a while, I knew he had different plans for me, not the ones that were mutual.

It was 2014, and till now all I did was run into him. I felt like I was being punished. I drove a cab for a part-time job.

On May 30, 2015, around 7:00 p.m., I was driving east on Fillmore Street. I saw him driving behind me. He was about three car spaces behind me. As I was getting into the turn lane to go south on North Nevada, he sped up and came within a few inches of hitting or more likely taking the driver's side of my cab while driving beside me. You could tell he was trying his best to do so.

I could not believe he did that. I was in a deep shock. Of course, that is not the last of him doing that. On July 31, 2015, at about 9:30 p.m., I picked up two people at the Greyhound station. I asked where they wanted to go. They gave me an address of a hotel up in Denver, near the airport. I got them there between 10:45 p.m. and 11:00 p.m.

They paid and got on their way. At about 11:00 p.m., I finally left the hotel to make it back to Colorado Springs. I was now driving on Highway 225, going west. I was about three miles away from 1-25, so I could go south to get back to the Springs, so I could do the bar rush.

No more than a half mile down the road, I got this truck smack-dab on the rear end of my cab, flashing its light off and on. I looked up through the back window through my mirror and noticed the truck right off the bat, then he switched lanes. I was driving in the middle lane, so he switched to the lane on the right side of me, and I was not surprised to see Mark S. beside me. I sped up some, then he sped up as well, just to look at me, the same damn look that he always gave, but it scared me even more. He drove beside me for about ten miles. I tried not to look at him, so I watched him from the corner of my eye. I saw him pushing himself into my lane while I was beside him. Yes, he was trying to hit me or make it a point to push me and my car into the cement wall.

So, I started to speed up so I could get rid of him. I got ahead of him to where I could get in front of him, then he moved to the lane I was in so he could speed up to get alongside me again. Finally, there were more cars around us, so it kind of made it hard for him to do anything.

He was playing this dumb, stupid game with me for over an hour. I don't really know what he was going to gain by trying to hurt me or kill me. All he was doing was getting himself deeper into his shity lifestyle he put himself into.
Anything he had done wrong in his life he blamed me or others, to help him not take responsibility for it. I know he will never change.

With all the heartaches he had put me through since the day I met him, it caused part of me to die. He took that part of my life that I had. I'm feeling less complete. I can't heal. He has not yet let me go. I feel the strain of needing to be let go.

Everything that happened goes through my mind like a movie on a projector. It goes in circles. It won't let go; it won't go away. I still go to see the counselor to this day. I'm still having a hard time dealing with it.

In August of 2014, I was diagnosed with clinical depression, anxiety, and PTSD from all the stuff he had done to me over the years. Having to go through all this is debilitating. My advice to any woman is if you have some bad feelings deep down inside your gut about the man or the friend you're with, even if you are dating the person, if they're not acting right, then leave them. It's not worth it being around them.

I was scared when I left, and almost four years later, I'm still terrified of him doing something physical to me. Seek some help at your nearest crisis office. Because the man did bad things to me, in my heart. He has lots of problems. I'm trying to learn how to not let people like him take me over like he did. He is very manipulative. People like that are very skillful, and controlling. When you say something, they make you feel very guilty about it. They also consistently attempt to make personal gains at others' expense by means of manipulation. He does this really well. That is how he wins control over anyone.

Along with the manipulation, he conducts himself really well. He is a well-liked person because of his charm. He does not care about other people. He thinks mainly of himself and usually blames others for the things that he does. He has complete disregard for rules and lies constantly. He seldom feels guilty or learns from his punishments.

The way he acts, I'm surprised he has not murdered someone. He does not reveal his guilty ways to anyone. My counselor and I talk about the way he acts. She tells me he is not going to change. After she says that, I can see what she is talking about, but of course, I will never understand him.

She tells me there are lots of people out there that have problems just like he does. He blames me for being in trouble with the law. Well, that is a small piece of his problem. He thought I would understand and not get mad. Wrong.

Just being around some people, you really can't tell if they have some real problems. I really don't feel sorry for him or what he does wrong with his life. I feel sorry for anyone that crosses his path. I really don't understand how his wife doesn't see what he is doing. Maybe she does know but doesn't care, or she could be scared of him as well.

Since the last time he raped me, and I'd seen him, I have had nothing but fear built up inside. I have no way of controlling it. When I was around him, it was easy to read into him, what he might be thinking of doing to me or someone else. Now I can't figure it out or even know what he is thinking.

What concerns me now is his mental state. It seems a little more bizarre. This would be my feelings when I see him on the streets while driving around, 'cause of the crazy acts of hate toward me.

This part of my story comes to an end. Till next time, but when it comes to people's bad behaviors and evil doings, karma will come around and hit them threefold.

And to all my fellow women in my country and around the world, please, if any man does this stuff to you or worse, please try to get away. I know how you feel. You're scared, but realize he is not worth the pain he puts you in, He eats off it, and he loves it. Inside you're a better woman and person. There is help out there. All you have to do is go get it.

POEMS

DUSTINA RESPECKI

Not the Same Person

I know longer sleep the same, Walk the same, Or talk the same,
Or even dream the same, When I close my eyes,
All I see is you, and it scares me, I feel so nasty,
My body trembles down to the ground, Tell me... was it nice, was it good?
I felt you thrusting, I felt it all,
I no longer feel comfortable in my own body, Because you forced yourself inside me,
You raped me and demolished my safe place, My soul, my mind is going in circles,
Trying to find my secrets,
And thoughts, my body is trying so hard, But you invaded my personal space,
It won't feel the same, You raped me,
And you tell me I made a wrong choice, I was not in my right state of mind,
From all the abuse,
You forced me alone in a room or behind a car, I don't want you, I curled up on a cold floor in pain, In rage,
You have invaded and created fear in me, It seems to haunt me day and night, Because now I can't sleep well,
All I ask is for you to leave my mind, Let my soul free,
Please let my body rest,
Forgive me for feeling this way, but you made me this way, I'm no longer the same woman,
As I go with in myself, And now I'm lost,
I scream from the inside out, When will it stop?

Forever Changed

I heard the footsteps coming,
And I knew this would be another long night,
And something inside me screamed, "This time it really isn't right," The
words he was saying were ruthless and cruel,
And each time he lashed at me with abuse, I sat there and obeyed each
and very rule,
I sat there blank faced,
And scared knowing that I couldn't cry,
For I knew what would happen if he saw the tears in my eyes, Each
and every swing of hate, I felt worse and worse,
He pushed me against the wall,
Then proceeded to pin me to the ground, He would not let me make a
sound,
I started to struggle and tried to release myself of his forceful grip, The
next thing I heard was a loud, horrifying rip,
His hands were cold at first touch,
I don't understand how a man could hate a woman so much, I froze, I
just kept looking at the clock, wanting him to be gone, I tried so badly
not to think of the sharp pain,
I closed my eyes, wishing the time would just pass by, He would push
harder and harder,
Disgust was all I felt,
Something happened inside of me that I cannot explain, I got this surge
of energy and said, "I hate you," Somehow some way, I got out just in
time,
But what he had already done will never get out of my mind, From
then on, my life has been forever changed,
It was like all I knew had been rearranged, Everything I have in me,
And one day I will end this war.

All alone

All alone I sit and cry,
I wonder why I can't let myself die, I lie in bed, covering my head, The marks he leaves are red, but inside I'm already dead, I hope tonight he just leaves me alone,
So here in silence, I may weep, Every day I clean and clean, He gets more and more mean,
He comes to me, and I feel I'm doomed, I wish I could run, Run from what he calls "fun," but the torture has just begun, Sometimes I wish I had his gun; I wish he was gone,
I wish he had never done wrong, I wish I could be alone,
Or just run from home,
But home is all I've ever known, I can never be alone,
He is always there, ready to tear me up, And I'm always here, full of fears and tears.

Not Yet

He comes into my bedroom in the middle of the night, I close my eyes while my heart beats in fright,

I feel his hand come tightly over my mouth, I want to scream, but I can't shout,

He yanks off my clothes as if they're paper, And when he begins, I think to myself,

"It's time to meet your maker,"

It seems like eternity even though it is a mere hour,

I race to the bathroom and try to wash away the pain in the shower,

The next morning, he packs up his bag to catch his train,

But before he leaves, he comes back into my bedroom and does it again,

I sit there feeling alone and ashamed, Knowing there's no one else to blame,

I know he will be back in a week, and to him he must feel like he is on a winning streak,

My husband doesn't notice what this man has done,

He doesn't ask if I'm OK,

It's like he doesn't really care,

Lost for words, it just seems like he is in on it.

This is a book about a woman who met this man at work. He preyed on her like an animal to get what he wanted from her. He earned her trust on top of everything. She had a hard time getting away from him. Now she is away from him; it puts her into a deep clinical depression from all the trauma he put her through, along with mental abuse. Now years later, she is having a hard time getting on with her life when she always feels that he might be around the corner, waiting. She has to watch her back alone to keep herself safe in the city she lives in. He still walks the streets, finding ways to get even with her, even if it means killing her. He has come close a time or two.

ABOUT THE AUTHOR

Dusty Respecki is originally from Denver, Colorado. When she was five years old, she left Denver and went to Hawaii to live. She lived there for over two years, then when she was eight years old, she left Hawaii to live a very short time in Texas. In June of 1980, she came back home to Colorado to live and has been here ever since. Dusty is married. She has been married for the last thirteen years. She has two kids, a daughter and a son. One day she was thinking about what she can do to tell the people about people like Mark S., so she took up writing a book about what happened to her so it.